694 E·IA

£5.00

Writers of Wales

EDITORS

MEIC STEPHENS   R. BRINLEY JONES

Felicia Hemans by A. Fletcher

Peter W. Trinder

MRS
HEMANS

*University of Wales Press
on behalf of the Welsh Arts Council*

1984

To the modern reader Mrs Hemans may be still a half-familiar name. Copies of her works in their many editions are still to be found in the second-hand bookshops. Students of Wordsworth diligently take note of her dates 1793–1835 as they come to the forbiddingly titled but very personal poem 'An Extempore Effusion upon the death of James Hogg.' There she is numbered among the poet's fellows who have preceded him *from sunlight to the sunless land*, as

> *that holy Spirit*
> *Sweet as the spring, as ocean deep;*
> *For Her who, ere her summer faded,*
> *Has sunk into a breathless sleep.*

One of her characteristically forceful opening lines struck the national consciousness so as to linger yet:

> *The boy stood on the burning deck.*

These are probably the real limits of the survival of Mrs Hemans. The student of Scott or Campbell will know of her, and in the lives of Byron and Shelley she provides a footnote or two. Time and

1

the changes of taste have not treated her with the tenderness her nature seems to deserve. Swept to a full height of popularity by a strong under-current of sentimentality that her own works helped to create, her reputation reached a peak during the Victorian age and seems to have survived among readers of poetry into the beginning of this century, and while the practice of recitation maintained poetry as one of the performing arts several of her poems were genuinely familiar among a wide cross-section of the public. Many a child piped aloud 'The Stately Homes of England', 'The Graves of a Household' or 'The Better Land'. When Kingsley Amis edited THE FABER POPULAR RECITER in 1978 he had a special word for 'The Graves of a House-hold' which he called happily *that superficially superficial piece.*

Superficial. So in our sophisticated and cynical age we could so easily dismiss the whole of Mrs Hemans; but we should miss much and I believe that it is more than the lyrics mentioned in the literary histories that we can find of permanent value in her work. Its sheer bulk is arresting enough. The idle browser takes down at last the title he has met so often, MRS HEMANS' POETICAL WORKS (or in the Oxford edition—for she is among the Oxford Standard Authors—more sternly, HEMANS'S POETICAL WORKS) and looks inside. He finds probably 500-odd double-column pages, a bargain at twenty-five pence. And so it proves to be.

The Collected Works first appeared in Dublin in 1836, the year after Mrs Hemans died and was buried in that city, though the 'official' memorial edition, edited by her sister, was published by Blackwoods in Edinburgh and London in 1839 in seven volumes including a Memoir in volume one. During the next eighty years several versions of the 'collected works' issued steadily from the presses of many publishers, though the most common are those of Warne, Routledge, and Ward Lock. In fact it would be hopeless to attempt a regular bibliography. I have twenty copies and no two are identical in all particulars though several belong to the same editions.

Born in Liverpool and died in Dublin, yet Mrs Hemans has a just title to be numbered among the writers of Wales, for here she spent all but the first and last few years of her life, and all her happy years. She loved the scenery of her little corner in St. Asaph and its neighbourhood so well that, as she confesses herself, she covered her eyes when she finally drove away to Liverpool with her boys, and little Claude had to tell her when they were safely out of sight of the scenes she loved too well; she never recovered from the shock of the change. One of the founders of an age of sentiment, she was yet far from self-indulgent; essentially a dramatizer if not a dramatist in her imaginative work, she yet struck few poses in her private life, but rather bubbled with spontaneous vitality, so that this inability to bid farewell to the Vale of Clwyd is a true measure of her devotion. These scenes made her a poet directly by their beauty and indirectly as a perfect setting for the peace that surrounded her incessant reading.

Felicia Dorothea Browne was born in Liverpool
on 25 September 1793, the daughter of George
Browne, a city merchant and banker who also
served as Imperial and Tuscan Consul. Felicia
learnt German, French and Italian from her
mother, who had married in 1786 as Felicity
Dorothea Wagner, daughter of a Liverpool wine
merchant—of Italian family, in spite of his
German name—and consul in Liverpool for the
Venetian Republic. Felicia was a clever child
who read early and voraciously. Her memory for
the written word was quite phenomenal. There
was an occasion, clearly remembered many years
later by her sister, when one of her brothers had
challenged Felicia to learn by heart Heber's poem
'Europe', then newly published. From first sight
of its 424 lines she committed it to memory and
recited it perfectly within one hour and twenty
minutes. When she was nearly seven her father
retired from a failing business and took a house
near Abergele. This house was later knocked
down as part of the site on which the castellated
Victorian Gwrych Castle, so familiar to modern
holiday-makers, now stands. Both houses at
St. Asaph, where her halcyon days were spent,
still face one another across the Elwy, though
the dual carriageway of the A55 also runs between
them now. The family moved to Bronwylfa,
St. Asaph in 1809. This house was rented, though
later Felicia's brother bought it. Here the family
knew happy and secluded days. Felicia went to
London in the winters of 1804 and 1805 but
otherwise they seem never to have left their
happy home. Felicia did not like London, though
she was enraptured by the new collections of
paintings and sculpture which clearly contributed

their part to the strong imaginative life displayed in her poems. These were troubled times in London; St. Asaph must have seemed an Arcadian land. Here she grew up little troubled by the outside world. The distant drum called her soldier brothers to campaign with Moore and then with Wellington in the Peninsula; one of them, on leave from the army, was visited at Bronwylfa by a friend staying nearby, a Captain Hemans. He was considerably older than Felicia but a relationship between them soon blossomed sufficiently for marriage to be mentioned. Mrs. Browne—who seems always to have been the presiding genius in this family, certainly with her daughters—forbade so precipitate a match. When Captain Hemans next came home on leave, since the affection had not diminished with due time, no more objections were raised, and the records of St. Asaph Cathedral show that Miss Browne became Felicia Dorothea Hemans on 30 July 1812. Captain Hemans had won a noted beauty and a girl of spirit.

As Miss Browne she had already achieved two clear distinctions. Shelley's friend Medwin had met her while staying in Flintshire and had written of her beauty and poetical talents to his susceptible friend. Shelley apparently wrote to her directly but Mrs Browne firmly rejected the connection; so close did Felicia come to being the ill-fated Harriet. She was further eligible in Shelley's eyes as already a published poet, for as early as 1808 there appeared a volume by no means slim entitled POEMS BY FELICIA DOROTHEA BROWNE. This was a handsome quarto published in Liverpool for Cadell and Davies of London and dedicated (by influence of her military brothers) to the Prince of Wales as 'productions of early youth'. The Advertisement acknowledges the publication as owing to 'the regard and partialities of friendship, and to the hope that the poems may in some degree be rendered subservient to the earnest wish of the young authoress for intellectual improvement'. The regard is amply attested by the list of nine hundred and seventy-eight subscribers, including several members of the aristocracy. Altogether 1178 copies were ordered and the list includes 'Captain Hemans, 4th or King's Own Regiment (3 copies)'. The name of Thomas Medwin also appears. Critical attention was slight but the poems now appear remarkable as the work of a 14-year-old girl, though few of them were reprinted in the so-called 'complete' editions.

The varying moods of nature on sea, sky and mountainside as seen by a stroller on the beach within easy walk of the house at Gwrych inspired many of the verses. The sea in all its moods is celebrated,

> Yet smile or be dreadful, thou still-changing Ocean,
>   Tremendous or lovely, resistless or still;
> I view thee, adoring, with hallow'd emotion,
>   The Pow'r that can hush or arouse thee at will
>
> ('Sea Piece')

Tales of wrecks such as this coast often witnessed, the effect of winds on high summer clouds and the white horses scudding into Liverpool Bay merge later into the frequent image of Christ stilling the tempest. These early verses are

essentially occasional apprentice work. The titles
include 'To the Head-ache', 'To Experience',
many poems addressed to her mother or
brothers, and to family friends; others on the
local scenery. All these productions are highly
imitative, the work of an avid reader of poetry.
They would be more interesting had they been
the early exercises of someone destined to be
among the giants of poetry, but the truth is that
technically they do contain highly skilled,
ambitious and richly varied work that might well
have augured higher things than Mrs Hemans
was in fact ever to achieve. The mastery of
rhythm and rhyme, with an ease that never
distorts sense for the sake of form, which she
showed so early, remained constant throughout
her writing life. In the popular sense she is the
complete poet: the critical question will always
be at what points can we distinguish her verse
by the name of true poetry. Which poems move
us so that we must read them instantly again,
and stand in the memory as a self-contained
experience *sui generis?* If that is how 'Lycidas'
or the 'Ode to Autumn' might be described,
is there any poem of Mrs Hemans with a claim
to distinction? There is a dividing line between
the convenient terms verse and poetry, and
while there are varieties on each side of the
line, I take this line to be a distinction in kind and
I feel 'that kind of pleasure' (in Wordsworth's
phrase) to be experienced from true poetry in
several of her poems. But those poems must
wait their turn. There is much to admire in the
way of sheer competent versifying in this early
volume, exceeding the performances of many
mature and interminable poetasters of the

generations since Pope who had poured out their hopeful epics, their lyrics and discursive verse treatises. The metre preferred for the ambitious sententious poem is still the heroic couplet and this is the metre of the two longest and most pretentious poems of these girlish years: 'England and Spain, or Valour and Patriotism', and 'The Domestic Affections'.

The first of these two poems is marked 'written at the age of fourteen'. It is over 600 lines long. Certainly it is fashionable derivative stuff but one wonders how many girls of fourteen could now produce 600 lines of couplets in such an elevated classical diction with such a range of relevant geographical and historical reference and demonstrating such a grasp of a contentious contemporary issue: or how many in 1807, for that matter. The couplets are forceful and energetic, perfectly 'correct' yet varied, though the rhythm is mostly monotonously iambic. There is an energy and elation essentially youthful, belying the technical skills; a vigour that is more than slavish imitation; and always there is clear sense. Two passages will serve to illustrate these qualities:

> *O thou, the sovereign of the noble soul!*
> *Thou source of energies beyond control!*
> *Queen of the lofty thought, the generous deed,*
> *Whose sons unconquer'd fight, undaunted bleed,—*
> *Inspiring Liberty! thy worshipp'd name,*
> *The warm enthusiast kindles to a flame;*
> *Thy charms inspire him to achievements high,*
> *Thy look of heaven, thy voice of harmony,*
> *More blest with thee to tread perennial snows,*

Where ne'er a flower expands, a zephyr blows;
Where Winter, binding nature in his chain,
In frost-work palace holds perpetual reign;
Than, far from thee, with frolic step to rove
The green savannas and the spicy grove;
Scent the rich balm of India's perfumed gales,
In citron-woods and aromatic vales:
For oh! fair Liberty, when thou art near,
Elysium blossoms in the desert drear!

Energetic lines invoke a challenge to Napoleon which may echo Wordsworth's sonnets of this same period but no doubt more immediately reflect her own thinking:

Despot of France! destroyer of mankind,
What spectre-cares must haunt thy sleepless mind!
Oh! if at midnight round thy regal bed,
When soothing visions fly thine aching head:
When sleep denies thy anxious cares to calm,
And lull thy senses in his opiate balm;
Invoked by guilt, if airy phantoms rise,
And murder'd victims bleed before thine eyes;
Loud let them thunder in thy troubled ear,
"Tyrant! the hour, th'avenging hour is near!"

So early the skills of verse were highly developed in Felicia Browne. Most interesting is the control and sense of shape this long poem reveals. Always a methodical writer, she shows thus early her meticulous concern for the structure of her poems.

Of the point arrived at in this poem her sister Harriet remarks in the Memoir, *Trumpets and banners now floated through the dreams in which birds and flowers had once reigned paramount. Her two elder brothers had entered the army at an early age, and were both serving in the 23rd Royal Welsh Fusiliers. One of them was now engaged in the Spanish campaign under Sir John Moore; and a vivid imagination and enthusiastic affections being alike enlisted in the cause, her young mind was filled with glorious visions of British valour and Spanish patriotism. In her ardent view, the days of chivalry seemed to be restored, and the very names which were of daily occurrence in the despatches were involuntarily associated with the deeds of Roland and his Paladins, or of her own special hero, 'The Cid Ruy Diaz', 'the Campeador'. 'England and Spain', after publication, was translated into Spanish.*

This Memoir is, incidentally, the main source of biographical information, but it is frustatingly eclectic in detail and even secretive at times. The later memoirs of friends like Henry Chorley are more rewarding but they are confined to her last sad years.

Apart from her Latin lessons with a local clergyman Felicia seems to have been taught formally by her mother alone. Together they worked at French, Italian, Spanish, Portuguese and German. There was also music and drawing. The engravings which formed the frontispieces to the seven-volume memorial edition of her work were taken largely from her own drawings which in themselves are highly accomplished vignettes of scenes around St. Asaph. In terms of the contemporary notion of the young lady Felicia Browne must have been ideal.

Early in 1812, still under the name of Felicia Browne, a small volume entitled significantly

THE DOMESTIC AFFECTIONS AND OTHER POEMS appeared. These poems reflect some of the activities and the sentiments of this period in her life. She often visited friends at Conway, and there met Edwards, the celebrated blind harpist to whom she addressed one of these poems. Its second and third stanzas read:

> Thine is the charm, suspending care,
> The heavenly swell, the dying close,
> The cadence melting into air,
> That lulls each passion to repose;
> While transport, lost in silence near,
> Breathes all her language in a tear.
>
> Exalt, O Cambria!—now no more
> With sighs thy slaughter'd bards deplore;
> What though Plinlimmon's misty brow
> And Mona's woods be silent now,
> Yet can thy Conway boast a strain
> Unrivall'd in thy proudest reign.

She spent much of her time lingering and reading in the ruins of the castle, then a romantic pile, standing, as Harriet remarks, as it then did in solitary grandeur, unapproached by bridge or causeway. Here she first read one of the verse dramas of Joanna Baillie, a poetess who was later to play an important part in furthering Felicia's interests. This association of books with the places where she had read them, as with Shakespeare and the apple tree at Bronwylfa, or Scott at Rhyllon, indicates an imaginative if sentimental self-conscious integration in her experience. Some playful slight poems in this volume—and in later productions—show her sense of fun. Her enthusiasm for nature and enjoyment of the company of the family's circle of friends show that she was not always lost in a book. Yet the derivative nature of her poetry, the evidence of her sister's 'Memoir', and above all the range of literary experience shown in the epigraphs to so many of her poems, reflect an extraordinary amount of very wide reading. And this was a period rich in material for such experience for these were the years of the EDINBURGH and the QUARTERLY and their many rivals, with the Annuals where she was to publish much herself. It has been calculated that well over half of the reading public regularly saw these periodicals. Literature was in the air. Whatever else a girl of independent spirit could not contemplate as a career, that of authorship was made acceptable and socially respectable by the example of such as Joanna Baillie.

Captain Hemans took his bride away from her childhood home for he had been appointed adjutant to the Northamptonshire Militia. They made a home in Daventry in a fine Georgian house in the High Street of this small market town then at the height of its importance as one of the main staging posts on the London-Birmingham road. Until recently a plaque on the house recorded the fact that 'Felicia Dorothea Hemans, Poetess, lived here'.

She pined for her home and family, and fate rescued her as the garrison was reduced and the Captain became redundant, but in Daventry her first son, Arthur, was born and one later poem remains as a certain memorial of this time, a

sonnet 'An Old Church in an English Park'. The
church of Fawsley stands alone across the field
from the great house where Ireton and Fairfax
met to lay plans and where Charles I was hunting
when called away to march the dozen miles to
Naseby. Felicia may not have been aware of the
history of the little church where Fell had been
vicar and some of the Martin Marprelate pam-
phlets had been printed, but she captured its
rural atmosphere well. The poem appears in
SONNETS DEVOTIONAL AND MEMORIAL among the
latest of her works, dated probably 1833–4

> Crowning a flowery slope, it stood alone
>   In gracious sanctity. A bright rill wound,
>   Caressingly, about the holy ground;
> And warbled with a never-dying tone,
> Amidst the tombs. A hue of ages gone
>   Seem'd, from that ivied porch, that solemn gleam
>   Of tower and cross, pale-quivering on the stream,
> O'er all th'ancestral woodlands to be thrown—
> And something yet more deep. The air was fraught
> With noble memories, whispering many a thought
>   Of England's fathers: loftily serene,
> They that had toil'd, watch'd, struggled to secure,
> Within such fabrics, worship free and pure,
>   Reign'd there, the o'ershadowing spirit of the scene.

Perhaps the sestet of this highly wrought and
doubtless Wordsworthian sonnet suggests that
she knew of the part Fawsley played in the Puritan
cause. More significant is the fact that this house
in its quiet park would be, after all, the only
representative of the great English country houses
we can be positive that she knew well when she
wrote one of the lyrics by which she remains

known even now in the occasional anthology—
and in Noel Coward's parody—'The Stately
Homes of England'.

Coupled with the Fawsley sonnet is a companion
piece on 'A Church in North Wales'. This is of
Abergwyngregin, near Bangor, where one of her
sons went to school.

When the second and third sons, George
Willoughby and Claude Lewis were baptized at
St. Asaph on 14 May 1816 their father's profession
was registered as 'Captain in the Army', but by
3 June 1817 at the baptism of the fourth son,
Henry William, this had become 'late Captain in
the Army', and so for the baptism of the fifth and
last son, Charles Lloyd (later known as Charles
Isidore) on 20 September 1818. In that year
Captain Hemans (rt'd) went abroad and never
saw his wife again.

In the four years between their first meeting and
their marriage, Felicia had continued to improve
her mind and her accomplishments, and perhaps
thereby foredoomed her marriage. Whatever the
cause of the final separation, there seems little
doubt that the couple were not ideally suited at
the start. She was a noted beauty, but she was
also strong-minded and no doubt an independent
thinker; he was a soldier and a gentleman but
he was older and had been wounded in the
Peninsular campaign; his health never recovered
properly from the effects of the retreat to
Corunna. There need be no mystery about the
kind of arrangement this marriage must have
become when Captain Hemans took himself off

to Italy for his health in 1818, while Felicia with her sons remained in Wales.

Her short married life was fully occupied yet during these years she made a definite mark as a poet, publishing the ambitious poems, THE RESTORATION OF THE WORKS OF ART TO ITALY in 1816, MODERN GREECE in 1817 and in 1818 a volume of translations from various European poets. THE RESTORATION and MODERN GREECE are very substantial pieces of work and began to bring her serious critical attention, though the QUARTERLY waited until 1821 to comment on several of her works together.

THE RESTORATION celebrates in turn the centres of Italian art, particularly in Florence, Venice and Rome, welcoming the return of their treasures after the depredations of the Napoleonic era. Typical of the hortatory nature of most of this long poem is this part of the address to Rome:

> 'Thou whose Augustan years have left to time
> Immortal records of their glorious prime;
> When deathless bards, thine olive-shades among,
> Swell'd the high raptures of heroic song.
> Fair, fallen Empress! raise thy languid head
> From the cold altars of th'illustrious dead,
> And once again with fond delight survey
> The proud memorials of thy noblest day.

Many minor poets might perhaps have produced the lines, but the methodical coherence of the whole poem is peculiarly characteristic. On this poem Harriet quotes from a letter of Byron to his publisher Murray dated 30 September 1818

from Diodati, *Italy or Dalmatia and another summer may,
or may not, set me off again . . . I shall take Felicia Hemans's
'Restoration, etc.' with me—it is a good poem—very.*

Byron said of MODERN GREECE that its author had
only too evidently never seen Greece itself. In
fact, Mrs Hemans had never seen any of the
exotic places in which many of her poems are set.
Her experience was rather literary than personal.
Of MODERN GREECE, following so soon after 'the
poem on the Restoration of the Louvre Col-
lection' (Blackwood's), the EDINBURGH MONTHLY
MAGAZINE rejoiced *that each new effort of her genius
excels its predecessor . . . and leads us to think that we have
yet seen no more than the trials of her strength.*

MODERN GREECE generally laments that the
classical age is past. It comprises 101 stanzas
fittingly classical in structure, a ten-line stanza
with nine pentameters and a final alexandrine.
The tone and diction are of a subdued dignity
that had just the right note in its times:

> *And he, whose heart is weary of the strife
> Of meaner spirits, and whose mental gaze
> Would shun the dull cold littleness of life,
> Awhile to dwell amidst sublimer days,
> Must turn to thee, whose every valley teems
> With proud remembrances that cannot die.
> Thy glens are peopled with inspiring dreams,
> Thy winds, the voice of oracles gone by;
> And midst thy laurel shades the wanderer hears
> The sound of mighty names, the hymns of vanish'd years.*
> (Stanza 22)

Footnotes give the sources of the topographical

detail and show the breadth of her reading in the fashionable travel books to be comparable with the more noteworthy researches of Coleridge. There are some fine lyric stanzas of general reflection:

> Oh thus it is with man! A tree, a flower
> While nations perish, still renews its race,
> And o'er the fallen records of his power
> Spreads in wild pomp, or smiles in fairy grace,
> The laurel shoots when those have pass'd away,
> Once rivals for its crown, the brave, the free;
> The rose is flourishing o'er beauty's clay,
> The myrtle blows when love hath ceased to be;
> Green waves the bay when song and bard are fled,
> And all that round us blooms is blooming o'er the dead.
> (Stanza 49)

There is even a thought that could well be quoted now in defence of the removal of classic sculpture to the museums of Europe, for as she points out, the ravages of time and invading armies would very quickly have destroyed the statues on their original sites:

> A few short years—and, vanish'd from the scene
> To blend with classic dust their proudest lot had been.
> (Stanza 88)

Though she must have just missed seeing the Elgin Marbles themselves, she had certainly read of their electric effect on the London artistic scene.

Some of her characteristic TALES AND HISTORIC SCENES were written in this same year, 1816, though the whole book of them was not published till 1819. During this period she also produced a series of translations from Camoens and other poets including Metastasio, Lope de Vega, Tasso and Petrarch. Of this period the ATHENEUM remarked *At this stage of transition, her poetry was correct, classical and highly polished; but it wanted warmth: it partook more of the nature of statuary than of painting. She fettered her mind with facts and authorities, and drew upon her memory when she might have relied upon her imagination. She was diffident of herself, and, to quote her own admission, 'loved to repose under the shadow of mighty names'.*

The lyrics of this period, though not among her most successful, for not one is memorable, reflect her continuing enthusiasm for heroic exploits and her early reading of Scott. She sent him a poem inspired by an episode in 'Waverley'. Scott published her poem in the EDINBURGH ANNUAL REGISTER for 1815. But the next poem of any significance was 'Stanzas on the Death of the Princess Charlotte' dated Bronwhylfa (a frequent spelling) 23 December 1817, and published in BLACKWOOD'S MAGAZINE in April 1818. The Princess, only child of the Prince Regent, had died in childbirth a month before the poem was written. There is a family connection here but it is doubtful if Felicia knew just how personal it was: Thomas Henry Browne, her eldest brother, was aide-de-camp to Lord Stewart, British Ambassador at Vienna in 1814, and when Stewart set up the infamous Milan Commission to collect evidence on the supposed infidelities of Caroline, Thomas Henry Browne was a member of the Commission. Though the evidence collected was not acted upon, Thomas Henry had

18

served his Prince well and received a Knighthood in 1826; in 1830 he was High Sheriff of Flintshire. It is perhaps unlikely that his sister knew of the Milan Commission.

In 1819 Mrs Hemans was again in the full light of popular appreciation when she won a competition for a poem on the subject of the meeting of Wallace and Robert the Bruce. Harriet tells that *she was recommended by a zealous friend in Edinburgh to enter the lists as a competitor. The news of her success was no less unexpected than gratifying.* Apparently the number of entries was overwhelming to the judges who were *reduced to absolute despair by the contemplation of the task which awaited them, having to read over a mass of poetry that would require a month at least to wade through. Some of the contributions were from the strangest aspirants imaginable; and one of them is mentioned as being as long as 'Paradise Lost'. At length, however, the Herculean labour was accomplished; and the honour awarded to Mrs Hemans, on this occasion, seemed an earnest of the warm kindness and encouragement she was ever afterwards to receive at the hands of the Scottish public.* One of her rivals was Hogg, the Ettrick Shepherd—with whose name she was again to be linked in Wordsworth's memorial verses. Hogg accepted defeat more than gracefully, admitting that her poem was *greatly superior both in elegance of thought and composition. Had I been constituted the judge myself, I would have given hers the preference by many degrees.*

The terms Hogg uses are interesting. Elegance of thought is a high Augustan or late Augustan expectation still twenty years after the appearance of Lyrical Ballads and 'composition' was always the strong point of the methodical Mrs Hemans.

1819 was a year of triumph in this respect but it was also the year in which this strange marriage finally failed. Captain Hemans (strictly 'late' Captain) retired to Italy. Mary Howitt, later a friend of Mrs Hemans, has perhaps the most revealing comment on the relationship which now ended. In her journal for 18 July 1827 she writes, *I have just now received a letter from Mrs Hemans. She congratulates me, I can fancy, with a mournful reference to herself, in possessing in a husband a kindred spirit and a friend.* That penetrating aside, characteristic of the elfin insight of the Quaker authoress, tells us much. The Howitts toured the country, mapped battlefields, researched, wrote and prayed, always together. Mrs Hemans, when the Howitts knew her, was ploughing a lonely furrow, as William Howitt described her *rather a wanderer in the earth than a settled resident,* and though as Harriet said she would never speak of her marriage, it was clear that she had found no such kindred spirit or friend as Mary Howitt rejoiced in.

There may be a definable tone which is unique to Mrs Hemans, developing in her work from several marked elements in her early writing which mature into a singular combination; a characteristic style she certainly had in the apostrophes and rhetorical gestures sentimentally imitated by lesser Victorians and finally parodied by the Edwardian music-hall; but what most clearly marks her poems as they stand in the collected editions is the choice of the exotic setting for narrative. These are very different from the settings of humble life in Wordsworth— her form of 'romanticism' being more nearly akin to that of Byron or Tom Moore or even (though as a pale shadow) the narratives of Keats, to the Campbell of 'Gertrude of Wyoming' and Coleridge when independent of Wordsworth. She may be following the lead of Byron and Tom Moore in such settings—the Gothic novel and 'Vathek' probably played their part, and the authenticity, both historical and topographical, owes much to the travel books and their reviews in the periodicals, but the dramatic evocation of such episodes as those chosen for the TALES AND HISTORIC SCENES (1819) is peculiarly a mark of Mrs Hemans.

Tastes and manners change, and it seems unlikely that such pieces as these can ever come into fashion again. Or should we say that the whirligig of time may bring back the fashion and the taste but by then Mrs Hemans will be long forgotten and the whole thing will be to do all over again? Removed so far as they may be from us and our literary tastes, we should still try to read as they were once read these performances, so impeccable in their kind, if we would understand the enormous popularity of the author during such a long period. The sheer terrifying excitement of distant lands and customs, the challenges to test the human spirit, the moral nature of man and woman put to such trials as revealed the enduring qualities by which that spirit would survive; values of heroism and compassion equally inspired by a religious assurance: these figure largely among the themes of the poetry of the later nineteenth century. They are as evident in Mrs Hemans as those softer, more sentimental notes by which we also characterize the Victorian period. The expression she gave to these emotions

21

and values may be seldom memorable, for she had no great original gift and she knew it well, but they are there in her poetry clearly enough. And as for the change of taste and interest, the plains of Arabia or the streets of Palermo may be a setting for the same human passions and trials as the plains of Middle Earth or the highways of Alpha Centauri. After all, who has really travelled yet beyond our system or entered an alien galaxy, though many wander these fantastic ways in eager imagination and there trace the passions 'really felt by men'?

TALES AND HISTORIC SCENES contains stories taken from old and new romance. The first and by far the longest is 'The Abencerrage', a heroic poem in three cantos of heroic couplets varied with lyrics—a mixture which was particularly associated with Mrs Hemans and followed by other poets. The story is taken from Spanish history and concerns the conquest of Granada. It reflects the author's love of Spanish literature and is prefixed by a quotation from the voluminous French historian Leonard Sismondi (1773–1842) whose work was evidently favourite reading for Mrs Hemans. His sixteen-volume HISTOIRE DES RÉPUBLIQUES ITALIENNES (1809–18) provided her with many more ideas for poems and many epigraphs. 'The Abencerrage' is full of heroic deeds in the cause of freedom—no original theme, but one that was often to inspire Mrs Hemans, culminating in its extended treatment in her play THE VESPERS OF PALERMO (1823). In 'The Abencerrage' the narrative is obscured by effusive exclamations and a profusion of abstract

22

nouns, often personifications. In fact it is hard to see the wood for the trees in such lines as these:

> And Hamnet as beneath the cypress shade
> His martyr'd brother and his sire are laid,
> Feels every deep resolve and burning thought
> Of ampler vengeance e'en to passion wrought

The reviewer in the QUARTERLY judiciously praised the authoress for turning to the disciplines and opportunities offered by the narrative form at this stage in her career, and it may well have been a conscious motive, if one remembers the final words of dedication in her first preface. There is an imaginative extravagance in the descriptions, an excess of exclamation not fully justified by the classical setting in 'The Last Banquet of Antony and Cleopatra'. The epigraph this time is from Langhorne's Plutarch, but the true source of the poem should surely be Shakespeare. As a child Mrs Hemans had read Shakespeare eagerly and her sister tells how she would sit in an apple tree reading the plays. Yet the final incident in this poem is based on Plutarch's original account of the marvel heard in the Alexandrian night which foretold the fall of Antony. Everyone knows how Shakespeare dramatically subdues his version of the incident so that a few soldiers, changing guard, hear a sound under the earth. Plutarch, in Langhorne's words, calls it 'a tumultuous procession' and so Mrs Hemans takes it at the end of her poem:

> Wake Alexandria! through thy streets the tread
> Of steps unseen is hurrying, and the note
> Of pipe, and lyre, and trumpet, wild and dread

23

Is heard upon the midnight air to float;
And voices, clamorous as in frenzied mirth,
Mingle their thousand tones, which are not of the earth.

These are no mortal sounds—their thrilling strain
Hath more mysterious power, and birth more high;
And the deep horror chilling every vein
Owns them of stern terrific augury.

Beings of worlds unknown! ye pass away,
O ye invisible and awful throng!
Your echoing footsteps and resounding lay
To Caesar's camp exulting move along;
Thy gods forsake thee, Antony! the sky
By that dread sign reveals thy doom—'Despair and die'.

Perhaps her reading of Shakespeare had been selected or controlled. She quotes from Richard III in this last line but goes back to the original source (though Langhorne and not North) rather than follow Shakespeare's version of the Hercules incident.

'Alaric in Italy', the next poem in the series, is based on an incident in Gibbon, another of her favourite books. She takes the hint from Gibbon's account to mark the awful significance of the very moment of the fall of Rome itself. Gibbon says *At the hour of midnight the Salarian gate was silently opened, and the inhabitants were awakened by the tremendous sound of the Gothic trumpet. Eleven hundred and sixty-three years after the foundation of Rome, the imperial city, which had subdued and civilized so considerable a portion of mankind, was delivered to the licentious fury of the tribes of Germany and Scythia.* Mrs Hemans rises to the occasion in lines that Macaulay might have envied:

24

Heard ye the Gothic trumpet's blast?
The march of hosts as Alaric pass'd?
That fearful sound, at midnight deep,
Burst on the Eternal City's sleep:—
How woke the mighty? She whose will
So long had bid the world be still,
Her sword a sceptre, and her eye
Th'ascendant star of destiny!
She woke—to view the dread array
Of Scythians rushing to their prey,
To hear her streets resound the cries
Pour'd from a thousand agonies!
While the strange light of flames, that gave
A ruddy glow to Tiber's wave,
Bursting in that terrific hour
From fane and palace, dome and tower,
Reveal'd the throngs, for aid divine,
Clinging to many a worshipp'd shrine:
Fierce fitful radiance wildly shed
O'er spear and sword, with carnage red,
Shone o'er the suppliant and the flying,
And kindled pyres for Romans dying.

The heroine of 'The Wife of Asdrubal' is the first
of a line of noble women and the poem fore-
shadows a collection of such portraits in one of
her most celebrated and characteristic works, the
'Records of Woman' of 1828. Another poem in
this present group, 'The Death of Conradin',
looks forward to the subject of her tragedy, THE
VESPERS OF PALERMO. This poem, like some others
of the series, is based on an incident from
Sismondi.

The critical enthusiasm which greeted TALES
AND HISTORIC SCENES throws light on what was

understood by 'romantic' in the period that we call by that name. The reviewer of the EDINBURGH MONTHLY speaks of *inspiration—as it is poetically called,* and of *a vivacity and fertility of imagination,* but praises most highly the tact with which she combines these qualities with a restraint more classical. *The judicious propriety wherewith she bestows on each element of her composition its due share of fancy and of feeling, much increases our respect for her powers. With an exquisite airiness and spirit, with an imagery which quite sparkles, are touched her lighter delineations; with a rich and glowing pencil, her descriptions of visible nature: a sublime eloquence is the charm of her sentiments of magnanimity; while she melts into tenderness with a grace in which she has few equals.* And the reviewer of CONSTABLE's enthuses over *so much genuine talent.*

By 1820 Mrs Hemans had clearly arrived on the busy literary scene, but she was still living quietly in St. Asaph. The house 'Bronwylfa' stands below the town and is now but a shadow of the house she knew, having been rebuilt on a smaller scale after a fire in the 1930's. In 1820 she published two significant and substantial poems, THE SCEPTIC and STANZAS TO THE MEMORY OF GEORGE THE THIRD, as well as her only published prose writings, and met a man ten years older than herself whom the sentimental biographer might regret she had not met twelve years earlier. This was Reginald Heber who had married the daughter of the Dean of St. Asaph in 1809. A man of considerable academic distinction and great charm, a fellow of All Souls and marked for a distinguished career in the Church, Heber preferred at this time a rural rectory in Shropshire where he could compose his verses, his Dictionary of the Bible and his hymns—one of the best known of these, 'From Greenland's Icy Mountain' was composed at Wrexham. Mrs Hemans met him at the home of the Bishop, Benjamin Luxmore. Harriet's Memoir tells of the encouragement her sister received from the Bishop in her writing and notes that *the poem of 'The Sceptic' was one in which her revered friend took a peculiar interest.* The Bishop declined the dedication of this work, astutely advising her instead to dedicate it to Gifford, the editor of the QUARTERLY, but we see the delicacy of the authoress recoiling from the ways of self-interest, moved *by a fear that it might be construed into a manouevre to propitiate the good graces of the Quarterly Review; and from the slightest approach to any such mode of propitiation, her sensitive nature recoiled with almost fastidious delicacy.*

THE SCEPTIC is a remarkable poem in its subject and its performance. The subject is really the necessity of deism—an answer to Shelley, as it might have been had she known of the notorious 'Necessity of Atheism'. As the QUARTERLY remarked *Mrs Hemans does not attempt to reason learnedly or labouriously in verse . . . But the argument of the Sceptic is one of irresistible force to confirm a wavering mind; it is simply resting the truth of religion on the necessity of it, on the utter misery and helplessness of man without it.* The review is full of reasoned eulogy.

The poem must be read as a whole (it is some 500 lines long) for proper appreciation, of course, especially because its coherent structure is quite powerful in itself, but there are many striking passages and images .After considering the awful fate of the great and powerful who die without faith she recalls her mind to the 'unhonoured Dead':

> —*Hush, fond enthusiast! Still, obscure and lone,*
> *Yet not less terrible because unknown,*
> *Is the last hour of thousands: they retire*
> *From life's throng'd path, unnoticed to expire*
> *As the light leaf, whose fall to ruin bears*
> *Some trembling insect's little world of cares,*
> *Descends in silence—while around waves on*
> *The mighty forest, reckless what is gone!*
> *Such is man's doom; and, ere an hour be flown,*
> *—Start not, thou trifler!—such may be thine own.*

The sincerity of the poem's sentiments is quite unmistakable and confirms the strength of spirit with which she was to bear sufferings, as it foreshadows the calm assurance of her own last days. This assurance no doubt tempers the expression of the whole poem, restraining the extravagance fatal to such a subject. There is none of the mawkishness which would have betrayed a lesser artistic control, so that the nearest poetic equivalent that comes to mind is the familiar sweet reasonableness of Dryden's translation of the Third Book of Lucretius—which leads, of course, to a completely opposite conclusion and so makes an interesting comparison in the use of the heroic couplet for a contemplative poem—if, that is, one can recognize the frequent use of the exclamation mark as a mere convention of typography. It would be dangerous to assert what Mrs Hemans had not read, and sure enough it seems that she knows and dismisses the arguments of Lucretius a few lines later when she exclaims:

If vain philosophy, with tranquil pride,
Would mock the feelings she perchance can hide,
Call up the countless armies of the dead,
Point to the pathway beaten by their tread,
And say—'What wouldst thou? Shall the fixed decree
Made for creation, be reversed for thee?'
—Poor, feeble aid!—proud stoic! ask not why,
It is enough that nature shrinks to die!
Enough that horror, which thy words upbraid,
Is her dread penalty, and must be paid!

In this poem, tone, style, subject and form are so
well suited and controlled that among the poems
of Mrs Hemans it is certainly one of those that
deserve to be preserved. Perhaps her mind had
returned to Shelley in this poem. How she might
know of his youthful pamphlet one could not
guess but it is possible that she is thinking of
'Prometheus Unbound' and 'Ozymandias' as she
writes; the former was published in the same year
as THE SCEPTIC and the sonnet had appeared in
1818. Speaking of contemporary publications, it
helps to fix a poem in its literary scene to realize
that in this same year of 1820 there were published
Clare's POEMS, DESCRIPTIVE OF RURAL LIFE, Wash-
ington Irving's SKETCHBOOK and of course, most
notable of all, Keats's 'Lamia', 'Isabella', 'The Eve
of St. Agnes' and 'Hyperion'. Lamb's 'Essays of
Elia' began to appear in the LONDON MAGAZINE,
Scott published THE MONASTERY and THE ABBOT,
and Southey the LIFE OF WESLEY. Clare was an
exact contemporary of Mrs Hemans, having been
born in the same year, 1793.

A more ambitious poem than THE SCEPTIC,
provisionally titled 'Superstition and Revelation'

was abandoned in spite of the encouragement of Heber; as one critic says, *She could not give the necessary effort to such sustained researches. One regrets this for she had powers to support a flight of some compass, and amidst the multitude of her smaller pieces one longs for a greater proportion of extended thought.* At about the same time she contributed several papers on foreign literature to the EDINBURGH MONTHLY. These contained translations of poems and passages from dramas with critical comments that reveal her wide knowledge of classical drama as well as her sympathy with the nationalistic sentiments of contemporary Italian poets. In June 1821 she won the prize for the best poem on 'Dartmoor' awarded by the Royal Society of Literature and in the same year she was writing her WELSH MELODIES and her romantic tragedy THE VESPERS OF PALERMO.

The WELSH MELODIES are a mixture of imaginative recreations of scenes from Welsh history and translations of Welsh poems. The text is unusually rich in her own notes which explain the background in Welsh history, the etymology of place names, pronunciation and other matters of interest. It seems likely that she could read and understand the Welsh language sufficiently for us to accept that the translations contained in this collection may be her own originals rather than paraphrases, but if so they are for the most part very free versions. Following the researches and publications of Gray and Southey, among others, as part of the cult of romantic experience, there was a public interest in such titles as 'The Hirlas Horn,' 'The Hall of Cynddylan,' 'Taliesin's Prophecy,' 'Prince Madoc's Farewell,' and the

'Rock of Cader Idris.' The poems were written to be set to music and in these settings they remained very popular throughout the following century and well beyond, while parlour music-making remained in fashion. In this way Mrs Hemans obviously contributed largely to the continuing interest beyond Wales in things Welsh. To celebrate the grand London Eisteddfod of May 1822, she wrote 'The Meeting of the Bards' which shows that she was well acquainted with the rites of the Gorsedd and its history.

The Eisteddfod was reported in some detail by the newly founded CAMBRO-BRITON in June: *The Second Anniversary of the Cymrodorion was celebrated on the 22nd of last month at the Freemason's Tavern . . . The Anniversary may be described, generally, as having been devoted to three objects:— Musical festivity, business and conviviality. The first of these was the chief aim of the Eisteddfod, which took place in the morning;—the second of the General Meeting, by which it was succeeded;—and the third of the Annual Dinner in the evening . . .*

Soon after eleven o'clock the arrival of company at Freemason's Hall denoted the near approach of the Eisteddfod, and, before half-past twelve, that spacious apartment was already filled with a most respectable assemblage, including a considerable portion of rank and fashion.

The Chairman was Sir William Watkins Wynne but the leading spirit seems to have been Mr Humffreys Parry, 'Conductor of the Cymrodorion Transactions,' who gave *extempore, an historical outline of these national assemblies from the most ancient notices of their existence under the Druids, through the various periods of their revival by the Welsh Bards, whether as* Gorseddau *or* Eisteddfodau, *down to the era*

31

of the present auspicious re-establishment under the patronage of the Cymrodorion and the Societies in Wales. This being done, the same gentleman read a copy of beautiful verses, written by Mrs Hemans, for the occasion . . . To this would have succeeded the recital of some Welsh compositions in prose and verse, had it not been considered advisable not to detain the company, by any further preliminary proceedings, from the particular object of the Eisteddfod.

The concert later in the day included vocal and choral items as well as Harp and Flageolet solos and two examples of 'Pennillion.' There was an item on 'the newly-invented Cambrian Pedal Harp' and solos by Mr Edward Jones, Harper to the King. Among the songs, three had words by Mrs Hemans: No. 1 on the Programme (Glee and Chorus—'On the landing of the Romans in Britain'); No. 4 (Duet 'Owain Glyndwr's War Song') and No. 1 in Part 2 of the Concert (A Double Glee and Chorus, accompanied on the Harps and the Piano-Forte-Air 'The Welsh Ground' The words by Mrs Hemans).

Mrs Hemans would obviously have known through her own local clergy friends about those other active Welsh clergymen who were busy re-establishing the Cymrodorion Society in the early years of the nineteenth century. The movement began in Montgomeryshire but there was an Eisteddfod in Wrexham in 1820. The Cymrodorion Society in London was re-established in 1820 to direct and govern the Provincial Societies, most of whose leading figures were Members of Parliament and therefore found it convenient to have a central organization in London. The first meeting of this second Cymrodorion Society was convened by public advertisement and held at the 'Freemason's Tavern' on 24 June 1820. Many of the gentry of Wales joined enthusiastically; honorary members included Sir Walter Scott, and in July 1821 the Royal patronage was granted, so that *henceforth its patriotic objects were to have the advantage of being pursued under the favouring auspices of the royal sanction,* (TRANSACTIONS OF THE CYMRODORION OR METROPOLITAN CAMBRIAN INSTITUTION VOL. 1 1822).

THE VESPERS OF PALERMO is her most ambitious work, a full five-act tragedy though not intended for the stage. Friends—especially Heber and Dean Milman—after reading it endeavoured to get it produced, and such was Heber's influence that a performance was arranged at Covent Garden on 12 December 1823. The TIMES of the next day was eagerly awaited in St. Asaph but the news was bad: the play failed and there was no second night. The review in the TIMES is perhaps rather patronizing but gives a lively insight into theatrical conditions at the time: the writer had attended so many first nights that were also last nights; he speaks of *this very so-so kind of tragedy which wants poetry and passion . . . There is no fault in it—save now and then a little awkward arrangement; but neither is there, that we can perceive, any excellence at all. We never are in spirits enough to hiss such pieces as these; but they ruin us in snuff to keep awake. The acting of the play is rather indifferent.* The male leads, Young and Charles Kemble were commended, but the young Miss Kelly's performance as Constance was so bad as to provide a reasonable excuse for the failure in the eyes of the author's friends. At any rate, hope was revived in the next year when Joanna Baillie persuaded Scott to use his influence with Mrs Siddons to stage the piece in Edinburgh where it achieved some success. The correspondence with Scott and Miss Baillie, the reviews and notices of production, are fascinating but too detailed for the present slight sketch of the author where we should rather look at the play itself. Scott wrote a prologue for the play which cannot now be traced though there is a short piece among some unpublished fugitive verses of his which may be it.

Scott had already given his well-phrased judgement on Mrs Hemans' writing to Miss Baillie in July 1823: *Miss Herman [sic] is somewhat too poetical for my taste—too many flowers I mean and too little fruit, but that may be the cynical criticism of an elderly gentleman.* Mary Howitt made a similar comment in a letter to a friend *Her heart is right, but her taste is vitiated. It is just like her dress; it has too much glare and contrast of colour to be in pure taste.* Mrs Grant of Laggan, another Scots literary lioness, wrote of her *too uniform splendour,* and went on, *She keeps us hovering constantly on the wing, like birds of Paradise, for want of a perch to repose on.*

The play reads like the libretto of an Italian opera, but again once we accept the tone and style there is much to be enjoyed in the reading. The plot is well contrived and presents an interesting problem of origins for there is no indication of where Mrs Hemans found the story and characters. The central incident of course is the famous Sicilian Vespers of Easter, 1283. Sismondi's account in his HISTORIE DES RÉPUBLIQUES ITALIENNES is fairly detailed and one would expect this favourite historian to be her main source but she has contrived a range of character and incident which amplify Sismondi's account to such an extent that, bearing in mind her normal range of creative imagination in narrative, we must suspect a much more detailed source. Although the overt issues are national and political—the rising of a conquered and repressed people, the resurgence of an underground liberation movement inspired and organized by an impassioned and articulate leader—the real concerns of the author are essentially domestic and personal: family affection, loyalty and love. The leader, Raimond da Procida, is a historical figure; the central event in the moment of the rising against the French is faithful enough to fact, but most of the story with its ramifications of betrayal and mistake, retribution, revelation and remorse, is pure invention. Operatic before the great operas of this kind were written, like other aspects of Mrs Hemans' work her one serious attempt at classical tragedy falls short of one ideal and declines into a new kind of artistic experience, a kind which, because it veers towards the sentimental in tone and the overwritten in language, smacks to us of the ersatz. But it was worth a try on the stage and perhaps it might even be made to work as a play now, with some judicious cutting and re-phrasing. It belongs to the world of 'Lucia di Lammermoor' and the early Verdi—whose opera 'I Vespri Siciliani' has no connection whatever except the central incident of the Vespers itself.

Theoretically the business of the play is quite well managed. There is clever combining of complication with exposition in the opening scenes which show the state of the conquered people, both the peasants and the leading figures including Raimond, da Procida's son. The rebel leader, da Procida, reveals himself to all of them in different ways; to his son his appearance is a profound shock and there is a clever revelation of the identity of Raimond himself to the audience. It would be gratifying to know what Scott thought of the play after he had re-read it carefully, as he told Miss Baillie he would, but the matter is not mentioned in any of his extant letters to Mrs Siddons.

Stage directions are sometimes strongly atmospheric—*A ruined tower surrounded by woods* and *a lone cavern by the rock-hewn cross*—shades of 'Manfred'? Another obvious influence is Schiller's play DIE RAUBER which she knew thoroughly. Much of the dialogue is the worst kind of fustian, a rhetoric without full imaginative involvement, so that there is no energy behind it that can carry conviction. It is well done as an academic exercise but it lacks imaginative force; images are almost entirely stereotyped, both grammar and syntax often creak with constraint and lack flexibility. The thrilling impetus and continuing surprise which should mark a dramatic dialogue with pretentions to spontaneity of utterance are really wholly lacking.

The development of the action is severely formal, both plots, political and domestic, reaching a climax in the third act. There is some genuine character development in Raimond with his divided loyalties between his father and his people on the one hand and his love on the other.

This is quite skilful plotting with fairly simple elements and issues which remain unclouded—except by the often tortuous complexity of their expression. The phrase *Love is yet Mightier than vengeance* stands out as epitomizing what is evidently meant to be seen as the main issue dramatized in the play. Thematically the two women are symbolically counterbalanced in this issue as Vittoria pretends love to further da Procida's plot, and Raimond's genuine passion leads him into a false position of having at least a strong and credible motive for betraying the same plot. The names Vittoria and Constance are transparently significant.

In the following scenes there is a reversion to an air of contrivance. The scenes are too stark and the continuity too simple; there are no extras such as waiting-women to provide anything of a more casual background, no trivial talk and so no sense of a day to day life beyond and around the plot—no reassuring sense of the mundane to serve as a setting for the main action and characters. Mrs Hemans evidently read her admired Shakespeare in the contemporary manner—for his 'beauties' and thoughts, but not with an eye to his skills as a dramatist.

The whole play is too intense, there is no relaxation, no slack, but all under impossible tension; yet in its parallel plotting and its clever involvement of the audience by dramatic irony, albeit of an unsubtle kind, it has some ingredients of a successful piece of theatre.

The conventional grandiose style is modified in

some passages which must have engaged her more personal sympathies, for example the early scene in which the young lovers Raimond and Constance say a lingering farewell comes rather near her own circumstances and perhaps conveys a sublimated impression of her parting from the Captain:

CONSTANCE *What? What wouldst thou say? O speak!*
Thou wouldst not leave me!

RAIMOND *I have cast a cloud*
The shadow of dark thoughts and ruined fortunes
O'er thy bright spirit. Haply, were I gone,
Thou wouldst resume thyself, and dwell once
more
In the clear sunny light of youth and joy
E'en as before we met—before we loved!

CONSTANCE *This is but mockery—Well thou knowst thy love*
Hath given me a nobler being: made my heart
A home for all the deep sublimities
Of strong affection; and I would not change
Th'exalted life I draw from that pure source
With all its chequered hues of hope and fear,
Even for the brightest calm. Thou most unkind!
Have I deserved this?

RAIMOND *Oh! thou hast deserved*
A love less fatal to thy peace than mine,
Think not 'tis mockery! But I cannot rest
To be the scorned and trampled thing I am
In this degraded land.

—could this be the Captain, reduced to half pay? Certainly the following speech could well be Felicia's.

Alas! too deep, too fond is woman's love;
Too full of hope, she casts on troubled waves
The treasures of her soul!

He assures her that he will return:

A few short years
And we may yet be blest.

CONSTANCE *A few short years!*
Less time may well suffice for death and fate
To work all change on earth!—To break the ties
Which earthly love had formed; and to bow down
Th'elastic spirit, and to blight each flower
Strewn in life's crowded path!—But be it so!
Be it enough to know that happiness
Meets thee on other shores.

After the real-life parting her elastic spirit was bowed down and her favourite flowers are more often blighted.

One of her loveliest lyrics based on flowers was resurrected by Jack Squire in his LONDON MERCURY (vii p. 186).

He reprinted 'Night-Blowing Flowers' with the note: *Mrs Hemans' energetic verses, once so popular, are now neglected, as (for the most part) they deserve. But she occasionally wrote with care and subtlety and the poem we reprint should be better known than it is.*

NIGHT BLOWING FLOWERS

Children of night! unfolding meekly, slowly,
To the sweet breathings of the shadowy hours,

When dark-blue heavens look softest and most holy,
And glow-worm light is in the forest bowers;
    To solemn things and deep
    To spirit-haunted sleep,
    To thoughts, all purified
    From earth, ye seem allied;
    O dedicated flowers!

Ye, from the gaze of crowds your beauty veiling.
Keep in dim vested urns the sweetness shrined;
Till the mild moon, on high serenely sailing,
Looks on you tenderly and sadly kind
    —So doth love's dreaming heart
    Dwell from the throng apart,
    And but to shades disclose
    The inmost thought, which glows
    With its pure life entwined.

Shut from the sounds wherein the day rejoices,
To no triumphant song your petals thrill,
But send forth odours with the faint, soft voices
Rising from hidden streams when all is still
    —So doth lone prayer arise
    Mingling with secret sighs,
    When grief unfolds, like you,
    Her breast, for heavenly dew
    In silent hours to fill.

If her powers in subtlety were often limited it is
fair to say that she always wrote with care; and
this is only one of many of her poems that should
be better known. There are other interesting
poems on the same theme of flowers; 'Bring
Flowers' is a fine lyric and 'The Day of Flowers'
is worth special mention, partly because it is a

40

longer poem in blank verse—a metre she found difficult. The measure here shows careful work on rhythm and phrasing that is almost Wordsworthian, and the epigraph is from Cowper—another secluded life.

After the excitement of her contact with the theatrical world, her life settled again to quiet in St. Asaph. She was writing continually and publishing regularly.When Jeffrey wanted her to contribute to the EDINBURGH REVIEW she specified that her contributions must appear anonymously and added very practically, *With regard to the terms of remuneration, I have never been accustomed to receive less than ten guineas a sheet; but I feel assured that with you there will be no cause for dissatisfaction on this subject, and will therefore dwell upon it no further.* Her contributions to journals were generally signed with her initials 'F.H.' and no doubt she was paid at more than ten guineas, for the EDINBURGH at its height of prosperity gave twenty to thirty guineas a sheet— a method of payment which obviously encouraged the longer poem. In 1824 she was writing the LAYS OF MANY LANDS published in 1826. These again reflect her wide reading in history and travel books as well as poetry and are introduced by short explanatory notes which remind us how seriously she took her work.

In the autumn of 1824 she began her longest poem, THE FOREST SANCTUARY which she is reputed to have thought the best of her works. At least it earned the distinction, together with her 'Records of Woman', of a major article in the EDINBURGH REVIEW of October 1829. One of Jeffrey's more notable articles, this has the famous opening *Women, we fear, cannot do everything; nor even everything they attempt. But what they can do they do, for the most part excellently—and much more frequently with an absolute and perfect success, than the aspirants of our rougher and more ambitious sex!* Obviously this confident critical statement demands to be read as a whole. It is not all so controversial and does contain fine points of discrimination on poetry in general as well as glaring errors of judgement. The reviewer of THE NEW MONTHLY, where Mrs Hemans herself often published, caught the underlying sadness in her work and phrased it so: *Among our later female writers, Mrs Hemans is eminently conspicuous for purity of subject, grace, fertility of fancy and a mode of expression at once feminine and happy. She commonly uses imagery of great force and beauty tinged with that melancholy hue of thought, which, however irreconcilable it may appear with our general impression of pleasurable sensation, is undeniably one of its most obvious excitements.*

THE FOREST SANCTUARY was published in 1826 and describes *the mental conflicts as well as the outward sufferings of a Spaniard who, flying from the religious persecutions of his own country, in the sixteenth century, takes refuge with his child, in a North American forest* (Mrs Hemans's own note). Here are the elements which most often inspired her more weighty poems: the exotic setting, a background of religious and moral dilemma, the bonds between parent and child, the uncertain future of the exile. The personal note is strong in the passage in which the Spaniard remembers how his wife would not join his desparate adventure:

> *Not thus is woman, closely* her *still heart*
> *Doth twine itself with even each lifeless thing,*

Which, long remembered, seemed to bear its part
In her calm joys. For ever would she cling,
A brooding dove, to that sole spot of earth
Where she hath loved, and given her children birth,
And heard their first sweet voices. There may Spring
Array no path, renew no flower, no leaf,
But hath its breath of home, its claim to farewell grief.

(11, xxxiii)

She strongly imagines the atmosphere of religious persecution. Her own devotion to the scriptures was deep and sincere so that she is well able to imagine a situation which forbade such reading and severely punished any breach of the prohibition:

It is a weary and a bitter task
Back from the lip the burning word to keep,
And to shut out Heaven's air with faleshood's mask,
And in the dark urn of the soul to heap
Indignant feelings—making even of thought
A buried treasure, which may but be sought
When shadows are abroad—and night—and sleep.

(11, v)

The poem is in two parts and consists of 169 stanzas which are a variation of the Spenserian stanza less strict than Byron's in 'Childe Harold' or Shelley's in 'The Revolt of Islam' nonetheless it is a notable metrical achievement though as a whole the poem becomes rather turgid in repetition of a narrow range of sentiment. The Spaniard himself is no Byronic hero and the poem's interest is limited now.

In 1825 on the marriage of her brother, Felicia with her boys and her mother and sister Harriet moved to the house called Rhyllon, a quarter of a mile across the little valley of the Elwy. Here for three years, until the death of her mother, she spent possibly the happiest time of her life. She loved the garden, the walks to Cwm and the rocks and caves at Cefn. Her later lyrics revert frequently to these scenes, as for instance in a sonnet very well known in its day written in Dublin in 1834, the year before her death. 'To a Distant Scene.'

> Still are the cowslips from thy bosom springing,
> O far-off, grassy dell?—and dost thou see,
> When southern winds first wake their vernal singing,
> The star-gleam of the wood anemone?
> Doth the shy ring-dove haunt thee yet? the bee
> Hang on thy flowers as when I breathed farewell
> To their wild blooms? and round my beechen tree,
> Still, in green softness, doth the moss-bank swell?
> Oh, strange illusion! by the fond heart wrought,
> Whose own warm life suffuses nature's face
> My being's tide of many-coloured thought
> Hath passed from thee; and now, rich leafy place
> I paint thee oft, scarce consciously, a scene,
> Silent, forsaken, dim, shadowed by what hath been.

In another sonnet of this same series she addressed the river Clwyd—

> 'Long flowed the current of my life's clear hours,
> Onward with thine, whose voice yet haunts my dream
> Tho' time and change and other mightier powers,
> Far from thy side have borne me.'

Those 'clear hours' passed in the company of her dearest were prolific in the production of verse as they were full of domestic content.

Few of her letters have survived and those are largely scattered in the biographies of the famous people she knew. For example, in the auto-biography of Blanco White are preserved two interesting letters written from Rhyllon that clearly reveal her vitality and fortitude in a lucid and vibrant style. Her reading was as eager as ever:

Am I presuming too much in favour of the deep interests with which your history and writings have so long inspired me, when I make this request that you would sometimes allow me the gratification of hearing from you, and give me the privilege of consulting you on subjects connected with Spanish literature? (from a letter date 10 August 1826).

And again on 1 February 1827 she writes to him a long letter which he quotes in full. This has a deep personal interest as it concerns the death of her mother. She writes,

From her I had experienced an unremitting tenderness perhaps hardly good for me, since it is now taken away, and I am left to feel that this world has no affection which can fill its place. Still I sorrow not as having no hope; her life and death have bequeathed me too many holy recollections for this, and will I trust assist in guiding me to that better country whence she cannot return to me, though I may go thither to her—I almost blame myself for dwelling upon this subject to you, but my heart is very full of it, and the deep and true feelings I have found in your works have almost taught me to consider you, though personally unknown, as a friend.

On 31 March she writes to Mrs Pennant at Downing, again concerning her loss and the consolations she has found, but more particularly to thank her for her kindness towards one of the boys in entertaining him at Downing:

I wish I could give you any idea of the ecstasy with which he describes the wonders of the place. When he returned home in the evening I really thought at first that someone had been giving him wine which had got into his head, such was the torrent of words he poured forth and by which my head was almost bewildered. Breath at last failed him, and then pencil and paper were put in requisition, and he drew for me (or 'depicted' as he called it) the case of the mummy, the saw of the saw-fish, the jars of (?), the crocodile, Indian battle axes and swords of all shapes and dimensions, and at last 'the side of Mrs. Pennant's own drawing-room, all lined with beautiful birds'. His brothers meanwhile sat lost in admiration of all these marvels, and I had, presently, three other artists around me, all copying his extraordinary delineations. (dated Rhyllon, 31 March watermark 1825— unpublished).

In the autumn following the death of her mother her portrait was painted by W. E. West, at the request of Alaric Watts, editor of the LITERARY SOUVENIR who was compiling a gallery of living British poets. West stayed at Rhyllon painting three separate portraits, one of which was exhibited at Somerset House.

The LAYS OF MANY LANDS 1826, cover incidents and legends from European and American traditions and develop the exclamatory manner of the 'Vespers' into even less appropriate contexts. Yet there is a really imaginative attempt at a union of atmosphere and narrative content also developing through RECORDS OF WOMAN to a point where the finished poem is often close to the fine integration and economy that will be so celebrated in the dramatic lyrics of Browning. Several features of the later poetry of the century are latent in her verse with its far more modest achievement.

The RECORDS OF WOMAN 1828, reflect predominantly the influence of women as they are moved by domestic sympathies, most of all by the maternal passions which remain for Mrs Hemans the touchstone of human sentiment. Having lost her mother she becomes haunted by the fragility of her children's lives and the substance of these poems is often an evident projection of her own fears. The circumstances of her life, together with an innate and probably inherited tendency to dramatize her feelings, no doubt predisposed her towards the occasionally maudlin reflections and settings of much of her later poetry—and these are the works of such maturity as she was permitted to attain. In the tales which make up the RECORDS OF WOMAN this tendency is mostly complemented by a varied range of metrical effect and narrative structure. The achievement these poems represent in the latter quality is significant; there is an economy of narrative line reminiscent of the ballads and indeed she adopts that form in some of the poems. The metrical precision one comes to expect in her work is amply displayed; the versification may be unadventurous but it is generally preserved from monotony, and metrically she hardly puts a foot wrong; in fact, when she does let the rhythm falter it is clearly deliberate as in the opening lines of 'Pauline' where the uncertainty of the second line is justified by the context:

Along the starlit Seine went music swelling,
Till the air thrilled with exulting mirth;
Proudly it floated, even as if no dwelling
For cares of stricken hearts were found on earth.

A similar effect, similarly justified occurs in the
opening of another poem in this set, 'The Peasant
Girl of the Rhone', another attempt at the Byron-
ically flamboyant:

There went a warrior's funeral through the night,
A waving of tall plumes, a ruddy light
Of torches, fitfully and wildly thrown
From the high woods, along the sweeping Rhone,
Far down the waters. Heavily, and dead,
Under the moaning trees, the horse-hoof's tread
In muffled sounds upon the greensward fell,
As chieftains passed; and solemnly the swell
Of the deep requiem, o'er the gleaming river
Borne with the gale, and with the leaves' low shiver
Floated and died.

In this same collection 'Arabella Stuart' and 'Joan
of Arc in Rheims' were highly praised and the
last of the series 'The Grave of a Poetess' about the
fellow-poetess Mrs Tighe has a personal interest,
In 'Costanza' there is perhaps an even more
personal note:

Oh! he that could reveal
What life had taught that chastened heart to feel,
Might speak indeed of woman's blighted years
And wasted love, and vainly bitter tears!

So her life meandered now to an early close in a
gradual wasting sickness; but these last years

were filled by a restless movement. She left her old home in St. Asaph after the death of her mother and took the boys to be educated in Liverpool. She took a house in the village of Wavertree but complained of the dullness of her life and the locality, though here she made precious friendships, notably with the Chorleys and the Hamiltons who were leading lights in the cultural life of the city. The Hamiltons pressed her to visit their home in Scotland, so in 1829 she made the journey to Edinburgh, already important to her as the city where her play had succeeded. The Hamilton home at Chiefswood was close to Abbotsford so Mrs Hemans met Scott among other figures in Edinburgh literary circles. She seems to have spent some time at Abbotsford; Scott expressed admiration for her work and he certainly enjoyed her conversation, on the evidence of his Journal.

In 1830 she visited the Lakes and met Wordsworth. She spent a fortnight at Rydal Mount and took a cottage at Dove's Nest overlooking Windermere for the summer. Wordsworth's admiration was doubtless sincere but his pleasure in her company was not shared by all of his household; Sara Hutchinson at least found her uncongenial. At the end of the summer she moved on to pay another visit to Scotland.

In 1831 she moved to Dublin to be near her younger brother who was Commissioner of the City Police. Here she spent her last four years, moving house three times, sinking quietly in health and spirits. Perhaps there was little to live for: her boys were set fair for life; that was her great achievement, she had brought them up well in a happy and full childhood giving them the best education she could afford, supported by her writing. Two of the boys had now gone out to join their father in Italy. She was a facile writer of verse rather than an ambitious poet; her work was popular and sold well, bringing her a steady and mostly adequate income. She had always supported herself and family and now her work was done. With her friends gathered around her she died in 20, Dawson Street, Dublin on 16 May 1835 and is buried in the vaults of St. Anne's Church in that city.

Her biographer sister Harriet died in 1858 after sixteen years of marriage to her second husband, the Rev. W. Hicks Owen, Senior Vicar of St. Asaph and Vicar of Tremeirchion as well as Rural Dean. There is a tablet to her memory in Tremeirchion church. The old family house at Rhyllon seems to have served as his vicarage.

The poetry of these last years continues the themes and settings already established but her expressive powers are gradually more subtle with a finer delicacy of relationship between form and content in individual poems; also a nicer sense of appropriate length in treatment of emotion or situation. Apart from a number of significant lyrics, two poems in particular call for comment, 'The Release of Tasso' and 'Despondency and Aspiration'. The first of these poses something of a mystery as to its composition—few of her poems are separately dated. Harriet did not include 'The Release of Tasso' in her collected edition of 1839, nor does she mention it in her 'Life'. Blackwood's 'New Edition' 1849 does not contain it but in the same edition dated 1873 the poem is inserted as an extra and separate sheet out of pagination. Two other of her poems deal with aspects of Tasso's fateful career, 'Tasso and his Sister' and 'Tasso's Coronation' and she had published an article on Tasso in the NEW MONTHLY as well as translations of some of his poetry. Goethe's play TORQUATO TASSO was published in 1790, and Byron's poem THE LAMENT OF TASSO in 1817. As a recent critic of Goethe has written *in this period the figure of the unhappy Italian was the prototype of the poet menaced by his own genius and plunged by it into misery and disaster*. He became one of the archetypal figures of the 'romantic' conception of the poet. Mrs Hemans depicts him on his release from prison in Ferrara after seven years; he returns to Rome and there is the familiar declamatory opening to the poem:

> *There came a bard to Rome; he brought a lyre*
> *Of sounds to peal through Rome's triumphant sky*

We are on familiar ground with this style, but as the poem proceeds there is felt an underlying sureness of touch, more spring in the rhythm through variation of stress, an ease of enjambment, even with unstopped stanzas, that gives a sweeping authority to the whole performance, mounting in intensity until the 12th and 13th stanzas (there are 21 in all) carry full conviction and a sustained tide of emotion:

> *So deep a root hath hope!—but woe for this,*
> *Our frail mortality, that aught so bright,*
> *So almost burthened with excess of bliss,*

51

As the rich hour which back to summer's light
Calls the worn captive, with the gentle kiss
Of winds, and gush of waters, and the sight
Of the green earth, must so be bought with years
Of the heart's fever, parching up its tears,

And feeding a slow fire on all its powers,
Until the boon for which we grasp in vain,
If hardly won at length, too late made ours,
When the soul's wing is broken, comes like rain
Withheld till evening, on the stately flowers
Which withered in the noontide, ne'er again
To lift their heads in glory—So doth Earth
Breathe on her gifts, and melt away their worth.

The rest of the poem nearly maintains this level.
Two further stanzas justify quotation as examples
of sensibility lifted to poetry by the force of
personal involvement:

But woe for those who trample o'er a mind!
A deathless thing—They know not what they do,
Or what they deal with!—Man perchance may bind
The flower his step hath bruised; or light anew
The torch he quenches; or to music wind
Again the lyre-string from his touch that flew—
But for the soul! oh tremble, and beware
To lay rude hands upon God's mysteries there!

For blindness wraps that world—our touch may turn
Some balance, fearfully and darkly hung,
Or put out some bright spark, whose ray should burn
To point the way a thousand rocks among—
Or break some subtle chain, which none discern,
Though binding down the terrible, the strong.
Th'o'ersweeping passions—which to loose on life
Is to set free the elements for strife!

Such sensitivity to the delicate balance of mental powers, the fine line between sanity and aberration, she had already shown in the much praised STANZAS ON THE DEATH OF THE LATE KING (George III) in 1820.

'Despondency and Aspiration' was written during her last illness in Dublin. Her health had long been failing; her heart was weak, she had caught a chill and there was talk of dropsy at the end. Her last sonnet was dedicated to her brother on her deathbed. This longer, altogether more ambitious poem, 'Despondency and Aspiration' published in RECORDS OF THE AUTUMN OF 1834 looks back over her intense spiritual life and sadly recognizes her own limitations, while the beauty of certain passages proclaims her actual, if modest, achievement. The tone is again hortatory but better controlled than in her fully dramatic manner. She hears 'Prophetic murmurs' that warn her:

> *"Fold, fold thy wings" they cried "and strive no more—*
> *Faint spirit strive no more: for thee too strong*
>   *Are outward ill and wrong,*
> *And inward wasting fires! Thou canst not soar*
>   *Free on a starry way*
>   *Beyond their blighting sway,*
> *At heaven's high gate serenely to adore:*
> *How shouldst thou hope earth's fetters to unbind?*
> *O passionate, yet weak! O Trembler to the wind!*
>
> *"Never shall ought but broken music flow*
> *From joy of thine, deep love, or tearful woe—*
> *Such homeless notes as through the forest sigh,*

From the reeds' hollow shaken
When sudden breezes waken
Their vague, wild symphony.
No power is theirs, and no abiding-place
In human hearts; their sweetness leaves no trace—
Born only so to die!

"Never shall ought but perfume, faint and vain
On the fleet pinion of the changeful hour
From thy bruised life again
A moment's essence breathe;
Thy life whose trampled flower
Into the blessed wreath
Of household charities no longer bound,
Lies pale and withering on the barren ground.

In some of her poems there is an interest beyond the impeccable metrics and sustained within the careful progress of the prose sense. The inner tension which characterizes genuine poetry is latent, repaying study. For example, we know that her favourite season was autumn, and as one reads 'The Voice of Spring'—an accomplished poem in itself, like many of her extended lyrics—one becomes aware of an unexpected train of thought and imagery. The fifth stanza alone conveys the full sense of release and energy one would expect on this subject:

From the streams and founts I have loosed the chain,
They are sweeping on to the silvery main.
They are flashing down from the mountain-brows
They are flinging spray o'er the forest-boughs.
They are bursting fresh from their sparry caves
And the earth resounds with the joy of waves.

54

Accepting that the diction is conventional, one can still enjoy the lift of this movement, though perhaps the last line falls to an ill-judged personification too many. The shape of the whole poem over thirteen stanzas is satisfying; the shock of mild surprise comes as one realizes that the main thrust of the poem is not conventional at all: the imagery is not springlike. There are ancient graves and fallen fanes, wreaths, the ruin or the tomb, the stormy north; the voice of spring is a glowing sigh, the swan's dark note and the dark fir branch. The children of gladness, when they appear, are changed:

> But ye!—ye are changed since ye met me last!
> There is something bright from your features passed
> There is that come over your brow and eye
> Which speaks of a world where the flowers must die!
> Ye smile! but your smile hath a dimness yet—
> Oh what have ye looked on since last we met?

One might say that it is the ephemeral quality of spring that is being stressed; yet the voice has its own characteristic note, and it is a note of longing throughout, of unreality. Here is that inner tension which in a deeper mind more provided with a reflective range of phraseology, more original imagery and the sweating of more blood than tears, produced great poetry. Within the range of Mrs Hemans this poem is good enough as it stands. In fact there are a number of poems at this level which have much to offer to the reader and are well worth unearthing; the old second-hand copy is worth its price. A very presentable selection might be made from the enormous bulk of the collected works; it would include among others, together with several of the shorter lyrics: 'Despondency and Aspiration,' Part 1 at least of THE FOREST SANCTUARY, some of the RECORDS OF WOMAN, 'The Release of Tasso', THE SCEPTIC and one or two of the HISTORIC SCENES.

The poetry falls naturally into three kinds according to ambition or length: there are the three dramatic performances including the only finished regular drama THE VESPERS OF PALERMO the longer narrative or lyrical poems; and the short lyrics which contain those poems by which, if at all, Mrs Hemans is still known, such as 'The Hour of Death,' which begins:

Leaves have their time to fall,
And flowers to wither at the north-wind's breath
And stars to set—but all,
Thou hast all seasons for thine own, O Death.

If the fashion for reading poetry aloud in an intimate family group, or for the more public recitation, should ever return then she will come into her own again, for most of her work has that quality of immediate accessibility which characterizes the hymn or lyric for music. There is enough intellectual content in much of it to satisfy the curiosity without puzzling the reason; there is much to please the ear and generally an underlying structure to present the feeling of achievement, of time well spent in the hearing. It is strange that with all these positive if modest qualities she does not appear in any of the standard hymnaries. The truth is that her religious convictions, though no doubt strongly held, were not deep in her nature as it appears in her work. The figure of Christ stilling the tempest comes often to her mind as an image of calm assurance, but she does not draw on the more recondite regions of scripture.

She took her poetry seriously but practically, and her gifts were dissipated by the circumstances of her life, by the exigencies of over-production and the adulation of a concourse of uncritical admirers. She lived too much and too long alone—generally far from the springs of culture, and her contact with the brightest literary world was almost entirely bookish. Certainly she pursued her own course as a poet. What might have happened had she met the young Shelley is an interesting speculation. By the time she did become involved with the establishment in Scott and Wordsworth they had both passed the crest of enthusiasm and she herself was too well settled in her ways for any spark of new light to strike. The reactions of both poets and their families tell us much. Wordsworth at his most courtly was kind, but the bliss of dawn and the heaven of youth had both faded for him. Scott was settled into the productive respectability of the Waverley novels—Mrs Hemans was delighted to meet the original of Dominie Sampson who was equally struck by her—but Scott's daughters were hardly enthusiastic, thinking her decidedly 'a blue' and Sara Hutchinson was even more scathing.

Mrs Hemans was comparatively little influenced by any individual in the English literary scene, though her most obvious model was Byron, and in the literary histories she is generally classed with the school of Scott and Campbell; most of her works appeared while they held sway. Her debt to Wordsworth is more subtle since she does not appear to have paid attention to 'Lyrical Ballads' apart from 'Tintern Abbey' and of course she cannot have known the 'Prelude,' though perhaps it is likely that when she stayed at Rydal Mount the ageing poet who clearly took her under his wing and enjoyed her company in spite of some trepidation before her arrival, might well have shown her his work in progress which always included 'The Prelude.' The clearest influence on her career as a writer conscious of her femininity was Mme de Stael. She refers often to 'Corinne' and that extraordinary book, with its picture of the elevation of a poetess to Olympian heights, had wide influence among the London 'blue-stockings,' Lady Bessborough and her circle—to which Mrs Hemans was never attached, except indirectly through Jeffrey and through Campbell who published her work in the NEW MONTHLY magazine. Perhaps her independence alarmed the ladies of Rydal Mount and Abbotsford, certainly her presence intimidated them. She was classical among the romantics, being most impressed by 'Laodamia' and the severer side of Wordsworth. Strangely she was hardly touched by Shelley or Keats and her reaction to Jane Austen is nowhere on record.

Perhaps it would be fairer to call her sense of form a methodical instinct. At times one feels that it is a kind of artistic extension of the efficient housewife's urge to see everything put in its proper place. Many of the structurally organized poems do carry this sense of near contrivance, a domestic tidiness about them. Take 'The Festal Hour,' for example: there is the rhetorical opening, a moral question posed, and in the second stanza we sense immediately that there is to be a multiple answer whose parts will form the structure of the whole poem. Such a sense of form so often repeated and apparently so effortlessly reproduced comes to be felt as mechanical contrivance—the art that does not conceal art; indeed the characteristic that vitiates so much of her work is precisely this air of contrivance. She wrote so easily when there should have been more effort and further consideration. She has a string of metaphors and basic images to hand; the same adjectives are assorted with the same features of nature in slightly adjusted combinations so regularly, in poems whose subjects and themes fall within a narrow range of stock situations or emotions so often, that to close the book after a session on the lyrics is to have the distinct sense of looking into a child's kaleidescope. You take the toy and shake it, and the same glitter appears in a pretty, new arrangement. The prettiness, too, is evident in the poems; their pleasing value as entertainment has often endured; many of the lyrics sparkle yet, but seldom does the verse move the modern sophisticated reader to recognize it as poetry.

Yet this should not be the final judgement on Mrs Hemans. In the first place she made her living and that of her boys by her writing. In that, she was triumphant and justly admired by her many friends as by the public at large. One of her sons, incidentally, makes an interesting appearance in a rare book by another forgotten author. If Alfred

Austin's poetry is condemned to oblivion, his prose is still worth reading, and in THE POET'S DIARY (1904) he tells of his debt to Charles James Hemans as outstanding resident English expert on the art treasures of Rome in 1862. In the second place, the honour paid to her by critics and poets of her own day must be remembered together with her great contemporary popularity in America. Professor Norton of Harvard admired her work greatly and corresponded with her; she was strongly pressed to take over the editorship of a literary magazine in America. And in the third place her contribution in helping to create the popular literary taste of the next hundred years cannot properly be ignored, however vitiated it is now fashionable to regard that taste.

Those dusty tomes of her various collected editions are worth rescuing while they are still to be found.

Two further matters need some special mention: the range of epigraphs to so many of her poems, and the bibliography of her works.

The epigraphs are from a wide variety of literature, both English and continental, which must have constituted her reading. Most of the English references are contemporary, with a large preponderance of Byron. Her favourite among his works was clearly 'Manfred' and she never refers—as one might expect—to 'Don Juan'; other particular favourites were Campbell's 'Gertrude of Wyoming' and Coleridge's translation of Schiller's 'Wallenstein'. Travel books and continental histories are common. As well as

Sismondi and Mme de Stael there are quotations from Bossuet, Lamartine and other French authors and many from the Italian, Spanish and German poets. In total there are over two hundred separate references in her many epigraphs. This clearly bears out her sister's comments on her love of reading and her catholic taste.

As to a bibliography of Mrs Hemans, her popularity on both sides of the Atlantic for over a hundred years was such that any attempt at a full bibliography is quite hopeless. The British Museum Catalogue lists 34 editions of her works, either 'Collected'; or 'Complete' up to a conjectural date of 1920 and this does not include some of the most popular editions which are still to be found and several earlier selections. Blackwoods re-issued the seven volumes of their original 'complete' edition separately and frequently after its first publication in 1839. (There had been a 'complete' edition published in Dublin in 1836.) Blackwoods also published a 'Copyright' edition in handsome large octavo in 1873 with the interesting insertion of 'The Release of Tasso' in some but not all copies. That poem does not appear in the edition recorded by the British Museum as the latest of all, published by Eyre and Spottiswoode, 1920, but this edition is identical with that published in Edinburgh by Nimmo in 1901 and by Warnes undated. The other common Warne edition, issued in their Chandos Classics series, does contain the poem as does the Ward Lock edition of 1873. Copies of the Ward Lock, Warne and smaller Routledge editions are still common. Some contain an anonymous brief

memoir, and some a much more useful intro-
duction by William Rossetti.

The truth is that Mrs Hemans was a genuinely
popular poet, much read and admired by those
who aspired to be cultivated in an age just later
than her own. In this age of Tennyson and the
parlour piano, the popular taste for poetry was
hardly to be distinguished from the religious
cultivation of fashion. The ladies were her most
devoted readers, of course: Florence Nightingale
copied out 'The Better Land' for her cousin in a
letter; George Eliot wrote to a friend: *I am reading
eclectically Mrs Hemans' poems, and venture to recommend
to your perusal, if unknown to you, one of the longest
ones—'The Forest Sanctuary.' I can give it my pet adjective—
exquisite!* A lady wrote home from India, *Dear
Mrs Hemans, I dote on that book. She just said the things I
was thinking.*

She is a social as well as a literary phenomenon
and as such, as an indicator of changing literary
fashion, she claims attention. Whether she does so
in her own right as a poet is, of course, a matter of
taste. In all but the most strictly intellectual part
of that which we can ask of poetry she claims
attention, but that intellectual part has become
too much the touchstone of poetry, and the
qualities for which she was distinguished are those
now at a discount. Her poetry is everywhere
heavily charged with the patriotism and the
domestic affections which are dismissed as
narrow, bourgeois or self-indulgent today. The
moral framework of society, the background
against which a poet writes, the assumptions and
social values have changed to such an extent that

the undoubted charm of many of her best poems remains only a charm. Where there were tears there is often a faint smile of disdain in the modern reader. In short, she remains frozen within her own period and seldom speaks to the sophisticated poetry-reader of our day. And yet if we can pierce the surface jingoism of Kipling we should be able to penetrate the lace trimmings of Mrs Hemans. But when all is said she seldom perceives those trimmings for what they are, and only for brief passages in her more personal poems, when something deep in her nature is engaged, does she sustain a universality that transcends the differences which separate her period from our own. No doubt all gain is also loss and we could well regret that we find it hard to sympathize with Jeffrey's strong assertion that in her poetry there is *Scarcely a lovely picture that does not serve as appropriate foreground to some deep or lofty emotion,* but then perhaps we are less prone to deep or lofty emotions. The poem he uses to illustrate that remark is 'On a Palm-Tree in an English Garden,' with which appropriate combination of the exotic and the domestic this essay may fittingly close:

It waved not through an eastern sky
Beside a fount of Araby;
It was not fanned by southern breeze
In some green isle of Indian seas;
Nor did its graceful shadow sleep
O'er stream of Afric; lone and deep.

But fair the exiled palm-tree grew
'Midst foliage of no kindred hue;
Through the laburnum's dropping gold

63

Rose the light shaft of orient mould,
And Europe's violets, faintly sweet,
Purpled the moss-beds at its feet.

Strange it looked there! The willow streamed
Where silvery waters near it gleamed,
The lime-bough lured the honey-bee
To murmur by the desert's tree,
And showers of snowy roses made
A lustre in its fan-like shade.

There came an eve of festal hours—
Rich music filled that garden's bowers;
Lamps, that from flowering branches hung,
On sparks of dew soft colour flung;
And bright forms glanced—a fairy show—
Under the blossoms to and fro.

But one, a lone one, 'midst the throng,
Seemed reckless all of dance or song:
He was a youth of dusky mien,
Whereon the Indian sun had been,
Of crested brow and long black hair—
A stranger, like the palm-tree, there.

And slowly, sadly, moved his plumes,
Glittering athwart the leafy glooms.
He passed the pale-green olives by,
Nor won the chestnut flowers his eye:
But when to that sole palm he came,
Then shot a rapture through his frame!

To him, to him its rustling spoke—
The silence of his soul it broke!
It whispered of his own bright isle,
That lit the ocean with a smile,

Ay, to his ear that native tone
Had something of the sea-wave's moan!

His mother's cabin-home, that lay
Where feathery cocoas fringed the bay:
The dashing of his brethren's oar—
The conch-note heard along the shore;
All through his wakening bosom swept—
He clasped his country's tree and wept!

Oh scorn him not! The strength whereby
The patriot girds himself to die,
The unconquerable power which fills
The freeman battling on his hills,
These have one fountain deep and clear—
The same whence gushed that childlike tear.

Bibliography

MRS HEMANS.

Works (selected)

POEMS—LIVERPOOL, 1808.

ENGLAND AND SPAIN, OR VALOUR AND PATRIOTISM, 1808.

THE DOMESTIC AFFECTIONS AND OTHER POEMS, 1812.

THE RESTORATION OF THE WORKS OF ART TO ITALY, 1816.

MODERN GREECE, A POEM, 1817.

TRANSLATIONS FROM CAMOENS AND OTHER POETS, WITH ORIGINAL POETRY, 1818.

TALES AND HISTORIC SCENES IN VERSE, 1819.

STANZAS TO THE MEMORY OF THE LATE KING, 1820.

THE SCEPTIC, A POEM, 1820.

DARTMOOR, A POEM, 1821.

THE VESPERS OF PALERMO, 1823.

THE SIEGE OF VALENCIA, A DRAMATIC POEM, 1823.

THE LAST CONSTANTINE WITH OTHER POEMS, 1823.

THE FOREST SANCTUARY AND OTHER POEMS, 1825.

RECORDS OF WOMAN WITH OTHER POEMS, 1828.

SONGS OF THE AFFECTIONS WITH OTHER POEMS, 1830.

HYMNS FOR CHILDHOOD, 1833.

NATIONAL LYRICS AND SONGS FOR MUSIC, 1834.

SCENES AND HYMNS OF LIFE WITH OTHER RELIGIOUS POEMS, 1834.

Main Collected Editions

W. Blackwood and Sons, Edinburgh, Thomas Cadell, London, 1839, 7 vols. with Memoir.

E. Moxon Son and Co., 1837, THE POETICAL WORKS OF MRS FELICIA HEMANS, edited with a critical memoir by William Michael Rossetti, illustrated by Thomas Seccombe.

G. Routledge and Sons, London, 1873, THE POEMS OF MRS HEMANS with illustrations.

Gall and Inglis, Edinburgh, 1876, THE POETICAL WORKS OF MRS F. HEMANS with Memoir (anon).

Ward Lock and Co., London, 1878, THE POETICAL WORKS OF MRS FELICIA HEMANS.

Oxford University Press, London, 1914, THE POETICAL WORKS OF FELICIA DOROTHEA HEMANS.

Biography

Mrs H. Hughes, MEMOIR (Vol. 1 of Collected Poems of Mrs Hemans, Blackwoods, 1839).

Chorley, Henry F., MEMORIALS OF MRS HEMANS, 2 vols. (Saunders and Otley, London, 1836).

THE JOURNAL OF SIR WALTER SCOTT, 1824–32 (Edinburgh, David Douglas, 1891).

Lockhart, J. G., MEMOIRS OF THE LIFE OF SIR WALTER SCOTT, BART. (Robert Cadell, Edinburgh, 1837).

Bell, Mrs G. H. (ed.), THE HAMWOOD PAPERS OF THE LADIES OF LLANGOLLEN AND CAROLINE HAMILTON (Macmillan, 1930).

Howitt, William, HOMES AND HAUNTS OF THE BRITISH POETS (Routledge, 1894).

Hall, S. C., A BOOK OF MEMORIES OF GREAT MEN AND WOMEN OF THE AGE FROM PERSONAL ACQUAINTANCE (London, Virtue and Co., 1871).

de Selincourt, LETTERS OF WILLIAM WORDSWORTH (O.U.P., Clarendon Press, 1939).

Vincent, Howard P. (ed.), LETTERS OF DORA WORDSWORTH (Packard and Co., Chicago, 1944).

Lee, Amice, LAURELS AND ROSEMARY: THE LIFE OF WILLIAM AND MARY HOWITT (O.U.P., London, 1955).

Thorn, J. H. (ed.), THE LIFE OF THE REV. JOSEPH BLANCO WHITE (London, J. Chapman, 1845).

Austin, Alfred, THE POET'S DIARY, edited by Lamia (Macmillan, 1904).

Morley, Edith J., THE CORRESPONDENCE OF HENRY CRABB ROBINSON WITH THE WORDSWORTH CIRCLE (1806–1866) (Clarendon Press, 1927).

Critical

POEMS OF FELICIA HEMANS. A new edition chronologically arranged with illustrative notes (Blackwoods, Edinburgh and London, 1865).

THE QUARTERLY REVIEW, October, 1820.

THE EDINBURGH REVIEW, October, 1829.

THE NEW MONTHLY MAGAZINE, 1825 and 1826.

Ritchie, Lady (Anne Thackeray Ritchie), FELICIA FELIX in BLACKSTICK PAPERS (Smith Elder, 1908).

Cruse, Amy, THE VICTORIANS AND THEIR BOOKS (George Allen and Unwin, 1935).

Symons, Arthur, THE ROMANTIC MOVEMENT IN ENGLISH POETRY (Constable and Co., 1909).

Hughes, W. J., WALES AND THE WELSH IN ENGLISH LITERATURE (Hughes and Son, Wrexham, 1924).

Davies, D. R., BARDD A GARAI'N HEN CHWEDLAU (Y Ford Gron, Mai, 1935).

Jenkins, R. T. and Ramage, Helen M., HISTORY OF THE HONOURABLE SOCIETY OF CYMMRODORION, 1751–1851 (London, 1951).

Acknowledgments

Sincere thanks are due and gladly paid to those who have helped in the preparation of this work, particularly to the Staffs of Clwyd County Records Office, Hawarden; Clwyd County library Headquarters, Mold and Ruthin; Warwickshire County Records Office; Cardiff Central Library; The Picton Library, Liverpool; Scottish National Library, Edinburgh; and St. Deiniol's Library, Hawarden.

I am glad to acknowledge an individual debt to the help of Mrs V. Dodd of Rhyllon, St. Asaph; Dr J. C. Corson of Galashiels; and especially to Dr Margaret Maison of Boars Hill, Oxford.

Materials for biography are widely scattered; there must be a great deal which this slight sketch has not touched, particularly in Dublin. There is as yet no full published biography of Mrs Hemans.

The Author

Peter Trinder was educated at Daventry Grammar School, Northamptonshire, and at Exeter College, Oxford, where he studied with Nevill Coghill and Jonathan Wordsworth. He has been teaching English at various schools in North Wales for twenty years as well as lecturing for the WEA and for the Extra-Mural Department of the University College of North Wales, Bangor. His interest in Mrs Hemans was stimulated by the common link between Daventry and Clwyd, and the present essay owes much to the interest shown by the WEA class of Mancot.

*This Edition
designed by Jeff Clements,
is set in Monotype Spectrum 12 Didot on 13 point
and printed on Basingwerk Parchment by
Qualitex Printing Limited, Cardiff*

It is limited to 1000 copies of which this is

Copy No. 0412

British Library Cataloguing in Publication Data

Trinder, P. W.
   Mrs Hemans.—(Writers of Wales, ISSN 0141–5050)
   1. Hemans, *Mrs*—Criticism and interpretation
   I. Title   II. Series
   821′. 7   PR4781
   ISBN 0–7083–0869–4